Loving from the Soul

Dedication

This book is dedicated to my amazing cat Pebble, who left this life on 8th September 2018 aged almost 21 years (100 in cat years!). She was my constant, faithful companion for all of that time. She was a very wise soul and the comfort she gave to me throughout her life helped make this book (and many other things) possible.

I would also like to thank all those who have inspired and encouraged my writing over the years, with special thanks to Mum, Philip, Dad, Brian, Claire and Celia for always believing in me.

Loving
from the Soul

A Collection of Poems

Sarah Caddick

SUNRAY HOUSE PUBLISHING

British Library Cataloguing in Publication Data
A catalogue record for this book is available from the British Library.

ISBN 978-1-9996762-0-9

Typeset by Amolibros, Milverton, Somerset, www.amolibros.co.uk
This book production has been managed by Amolibros
Printed and bound by Lightning Source

Contents

Foreword

Loving from the Soul

These poems are a journey through some of the highs and lows of my life during the last twenty five years. Some poems are factual and others fictional, inspired by someone or something I've seen or heard. They explore love, relationships, health, illness and spiritual beliefs.

I have had ME for the last eighteen years and at times been very restricted in my life. I find poetry is a wonderful therapy for expressing feelings and encouraging healing through finding your own truth.

When we open our hearts to love, we become vulnerable. We can be hurt and feel intense pain. Yet it is only by opening ourselves to love that we can experience the wonderful magic of intimacy and closeness with another. Maybe the answer lies in connecting to the deep spiritual love of the Universe/ God. When we experience loving another from this vast sea of unconditional love, maybe we are loving from the soul?

I hope that my writing may resonate with your experiences of love and life. Perhaps comfort or inspire you, or maybe just bring a smile to your face.

About Sarah

Sarah Diane Caddick was born in 1964 in West Bromwich, West Midlands. She began writing poetry at an early age, and encouraged by her parents, won a poetry competition at five years old. Sarah studied in York and gained a BA Hons in Drama and French. She then decided to train to be an infant teacher, and achieved a PGCE in Northampton, specialising in music.

In 1988 Sarah moved to Suffolk and began teaching at a school in Felixstowe. She taught all subjects, but was in charge of music, playing piano and flute. She also especially enjoyed reading poetry to her pupils and encouraging them in their own creative writing. Sarah was very involved in amateur dramatics and also played the flute in a local concert band. She enjoyed swimming, walking by the sea, reading, writing and playing Bridge.

She taught at the same school for fourteen years until, after struggling with the illness M.E. for several years, she finally had to take medical retirement.

During the last twenty five years there have been periods when the emotional ups and downs of Sarah's relationships and her health, have inspired her poetry writing more than ever. For several years when she had to spend a lot of time in bed, unable to walk or even to read more than a few lines, poetry writing became even more important. It was one of the few hobbies that she could still pursue. Sarah finds that it helps to

express her frustrations and transports her to another world, inspired by the beauty of nature, love, and her deep spiritual beliefs.

Sarah loves Suffolk – the flat countryside, the estuaries, the pretty little villages, and especially the sea. She now lives in Felixstowe and has recently adopted two black kittens called Roman and Sparkle after her dear old cat Pebble died. Her long-term partner Brian lives and works away, but is back every few weeks. Sarah's mum and step-dad live nearby and are a great support. Sarah has a rich and varied life full of family, friends, laughter and many interests.

Sarah has had poems published in church magazines and in poetry anthologies. She hopes that some of her writing may resonate with your experiences of love and life. Perhaps comfort or inspire you, or maybe just bring a smile to your face.

All the photos in this book were taken by the author except for the photo in chapter two. The two photos of Sarah were taken by Brian.

Chapter One – The Joy of Love

The thrill of first love, passion, excitement. The miracle of finding your soul mate. A deep growing intimacy as the years move on. Loving another can connect us to spirit.

First Love

That glorious summer we met
Long hot hazy lazy days
That felt as if they'd never end.
So many places to show you
Secret coves, hidden churchyards, deserted fields.
We adventured into far-off lands (only minutes away)
And discovered sights and senses anew.
Like children, we ran and laughed, rolled in the grass, dived into
    the ocean.
The wind in our hair, wild and free.
You awakened the wild child in me.

Tasting the salt on our lips
Hearing the waves, birdsong, stories from each other's soul.
Watching the world unfold before us
With intervals of eyes meeting in deep gazing as we consumed
    each other.
The scent of sea-weed, cut grass, wild roses, enveloped us.

Hands held, fingers touching, the soft brush of your cheek
    against mine.
You pressed a smooth Suffolk stone into my palm as a sign of
    your love
You picked wild flowers with promises for the future – a gift
    with three words "I love you".

We explored and discovered the world and each other.
Exciting possibilities stretched out before us like the flat Suffolk
    seascape.

But the Summer ended, Autumn came.
And you disappeared with your promises.
A wild child never to be tamed.
The stone still lies in my pocket with hope.
But wild flowers, once picked, quickly wilt.

Our Special Place

We sit in our special place
Holding hands
Holding hearts
Leaning together against the elements
Entwined
Everlasting eternal bond.

Cranes silhouetted against crimson clouds
Twinkling lights on the headland.
Our minds merge as we watch mauve magenta shades of purple
    in the sky.
Our thoughts gently float green grey white with the tide.
Our spirits soar with the seagulls
Our souls search the horizon.
As letting go
We become the clouds the colours the waves the water
And lose ourselves in this place.

We know every curve and contour of this scene
Yet always we come to it eyes anew
As we share the changing seasons
Time deepening our love.

Pure Magic

To have someone who craves
and savours the loving touch
as I do,
is pure magic.

To feel equal desire for
fingertips touching
hands holding
arms around enveloped entwined
as sleep overtakes us.
Our own snuggle-buggling language.

From big hugs
To the gentle stroking of an arm
The tender brush of lips
The deep knowing of each other
Gaze upon gaze growing
Souls merging
Love overwhelming
Becoming as one.

I Long for You

I long for the touch of your hand
To hear your voice is not enough
I long for your warm embrace
To feel your body next to mine
I long for your flesh in the depth of night
I long for your scent of sensuality as it mingles with mine
I long for the taste of your lips on mine
I long for your warm breath against my skin.

I long for the essence of you
I long for the depth of you
I long for communion with you
Soul meets soul
I long for the whole of you.

Reassurance

You stood in the doorway and at that moment your smile
  radiated across my whole world.
You pulled me close and at that moment I felt so loved and
  wanted.
You held me so tenderly in your arms and at that moment I
  felt so special to you.
You stroked my hair and kissed away my tears so gently and at
  that moment I knew I meant so much to you.
You told me not to worry and at that moment I felt so safe
  and protected.

As you embraced and caressed me with such tender passion,
  you showed me what you dare not put into words.
And at that moment I loved you so much
and believed that
you loved me.

Miracle

It's truly amazing!
A few weeks ago
We didn't even know
That each other existed.

And now
It's as if
We don't exist
Without each other.
Or at least
We don't ever want to.

Remembering Our First Weekend

I take a deep breath
My head buried into the collar of the bath robe, the one that
    you borrowed,
The scent of your cologne sends my head spinning
And my knees buckle as I close my eyes and once again feel
    your soft lips pressed against mine.
I taste the passion of your embrace as I feel strong arms around
    me.
In my mind I look deeply into your eyes and recognise every
    shade of colour – windows to the soul – as you look back
    into mine and we touch eternity.
I remember the twinkling glances of shared secrets across the
    table after only knowing each other a few hours.
In company with friends known for years,
Yet the bond I felt was with you and me.

My mouth breaks into a smile as I think of certain moments;
Your hand on my leg in the restaurant and the car,
Our fingers entwined under the sleeping-bag,
Your lips exploring my body in the dead of night,
Our tongues making their own special dance together in the
    secret space where two mouths become one.
I take another deep breath of the scent of the memory of you
And I wonder if it will last until the next time you hold me in
    your arms again.
But every day that it fades
Is a day nearer to the reality of you,
When I'll no longer need my imaginings
To feed my passion
For you.

Waiting

As I sit in your car and watch you walk back towards me
Time stops for a moment.
It is as if life has halted
And the split–second lengthens to embrace the whole of it.

Suddenly a feeling overwhelms me.
It is as if
My whole life up until this moment
Has been a preparation.

All thoughts, events, feelings
All I've done
All I've learned
Have been a pre-empt to this moment.

And it is as if I've spent
My whole life
Waiting to meet you.

Idyllic Carefree Sunshine Moments

Attentive to the senses.

The sound of a skylark singing in ecstasy
The sea breaking gently on the shore
Gulls screeching their greedy call
Your voice whispering gentle words of love.

The sight of your sparkling eyes loving across the lavish dinner
   table
Our skylark as we gaze at him swooping down from up high
The meandering estuary, and flat horizon pierced with vertical
   masts.

The scent of the sea as we breath in deeply embracing the
   Universe in Tai Chi
Luscious food brought to our table
The scent of your naked chest as we embrace.

The taste of your lips on mine when engaged in timeless kissing
Olives and smoked trout pate in the open–air
Gin Martini with ice and lemon evokes excited anticipation of
   the evening ahead.

The touch of gentle rain on our faces as we lie on the beach
Your arm around my waist holding me safe as the boat rocks
Naked arms entwined as our two bodies become one.

Idyllic carefree sunshine moments
The stuff dreams are made of?
Yet we've made them our reality.

Whilst others sleep their sleep of grey mediocrity
Or wait for some heavenly future,
We take a chance
And live our bright sunshine dreams.
Savouring our happiness
Nurturing our love
Breathing in each precious moment.

The Many Moods of Our Love

I want to curl up in your strong arms and sleep like a baby all
through the night.

I want to cradle your head in my hands, soothe your furrowed
brow, stroke your feet, melt away your pain.

I want to strut my sexual prowess as your mistress, empowered
with golden cords and red ribbons.

I want to submit in silken robes, totally beholden to you,
sublime as your concubine.

I want to float in sensual ecstasy on angel wings and cosmic
clouds, souls merging.

I want to writhe with red-hot fiery passion in sumptuous sex
with you.

I want to share my life with you and be as one with you.
I want to understand you and accept the whole of you.
I want to stay loving you and you loving me forever.

Early Morning

As I dressed,
Your look penetrated my being.
Your eyes at once glazed
And yet deeply connected to my soul.

As if in disbelief, wonder and amazement.
As if seeing me for the first time
And yet knowing so well every contour of my face and body,
    every thought in my mind, every feeling in my heart.

As if you could hardly believe the beauty of me, body and soul,
    that I was there
With
        You.

As if it were all a dream
And at any moment you'd wake up in your own bed
Without
            Me.

Out of your look poured such love
More love in seconds than some people have in years.

Magnetised, I came to you
And we melted in our gaze.
We were lost in each other's eyes
Floating in the depth of our love
Complete.

Your Love For Me

You took another poet's words
And they became sweet music on your lips.
Your love poured through the poetry
Like a tidal wave in a torrent of longing.
The voice and verse were gentle, tender romance.
But the flood of feeling was…… phenomenal.

These last days I've felt your love for me grow
So vast that it stretches out across the world
As far as the eye can see
As far as the mind can sense
As far as the heart can reach.
It encircles my body with strong arms,
Encompasses my mind with understanding,
Soothes my emotions with empathy,
Penetrates my soul with its very essence.

Overwhelmed, bowled over, I'm spinning, rolling, snowballing.
Confused, I lurch as in a pinball machine.
Maybe I don't deserve such love?
Maybe I'm scared to surrender?
Maybe logic observes too many obstacles?
Maybe the guilt is too strong, as right now your love is far
    greater than mine.
All so new for me……………
Maybe I need to lie back, enjoy,
And know that I deserve to have it all.

My Love For You (subtitled Heaven)

My eyes travelled the contours of your face
And I saw your looks change before me.
As your gaze softened
As your wrinkles disappeared
As the burdens lifted from your shoulders
As your eyes sparkled playfully
And your soul shone through.
Every cell of your body transformed into beauty
Physical perfection
At once an angel.

And the gap in my love for you was filled.
The circle completed.
I loved you with every atom of my being, every layer of my
    soul
And our spiritual union had begun.

The next few days it surpassed itself in physical expression
Love like neither of us had known before.
Fusing of physical manifestations
Joining together of souls
Empathy of emotions
Sheer ecstasy
Eternal oneness
Our true spiritual nature
We became God.

We were in Heaven
And how we longed to stay there forever.

Chapter Two – The Challenges of Love

When you open your heart to love, you become vulnerable. There can be pain, jealousy, insecurity, abandonment, yearning, unrequited love.

You're with HER again!

The Green-eyed Monster returns
She tears at my heart just when peace was reigning
She stabs at my mind and it is as if blood gushes from the gouges
    she makes
She bores holes in my head until I can't think coherently
She floods my body with an energy that's pure anger and rage
Raging red against the world
Wanting you to feel the pain that I'm feeling
Just so you know
She turns me into this selfish bitch—
The opposite of the Spiritual Angel I seek to be.

When You're not Here

When you're not here
The sun doesn't shine as brightly
The sky doesn't look so blue

When you're not here
The waves don't seem so calming
The pebbles don't feel as smooth

When you're not here
Jokes don't seem so funny
Food isn't quite so yummy

When you're not here
Ice-cream's not as sweet
Music's not as tuneful

When you're not here
Poetry hasn't as much meaning
Stories lose their plot

When you're not here
Going to bed isn't so snuggly
Waking up isn't so warm

When you're not here
The house is too quiet
And the bed's too empty

When you're not here
Life just isn't the same!

Interminable Waiting

Waiting
Interminable waiting
Painful waiting
Waiting for the phone to ring
Waiting to hear your voice.

Wondering
Hoping
Wondering if you'll ever hold me again
Or kiss me again
Or touch me again.
Wondering if it might be easier
To hear you telling me again
No way again
No hope again
At least then I could move on again
Get on with living my life again.

But I feel as if I've only just begun living
on a new emotional plane.
Never so alive
Exhilarated excited high and happy
as when I think of you and the moments we shared.

"Don't read too much into this"
you said as you fondled my bare breasts.
Not easy actually under the beams and the circumstances.

I reached the stars as you lifted me
I touched the moon as you caressed me
and your fingers through my hair

sent electric down my spine and set me spinning
across worlds never dreamed of.

Your words juxtaposed your body completely.
Which came from the heart?

How can there be so much passion, fireworks, dynamite,
Rockets exploding filling the sky with lights and sparkles and
    bright bright colour?
Between two people
If it's never going to happen again?
Don't tell me you couldn't feel it?

Waiting
Interminable waiting
Hoping
Wanting you
            so much
                        it hurts.

Wanting
Wishing
Hoping
Waiting
Interminable waiting.

Will There Ever Be Another?

Will there ever be another
Who reads me poetry with deep dark penetrating voice?
Who sends shivers down my spine as his soft lips gently brush
    mine?

Will there ever be another
Who makes my whole body quiver as he looks deep into my
    eyes?
Who sets me flying amongst the stars as he makes love to me?
Who makes me feel safe as he holds me – home at last?
Who makes my circle complete?
Who makes me laugh and smile in companionable silences?

Will there ever be another
Who turns my life upside down?
And batters me constantly in my mind
Who throws mud into my face?
And as I wipe it away from my eyes and turn
He throws yet more.

Will there ever be another
Who hits me when I'm down?
But only ever meant to love me.

Will there ever be another
Who lifts me to the heights of perfect passion?
And drops me to the depths of despair in a single breath.

Will there ever be another
Who loves me with such deep feeling?
Such longing, such yearning

Such depth, such passion
Such gentleness, such emotion
Such pleasure, such pain
Such a fusing of souls.

Who could not allow this miracle to continue?

Will there ever be another
Who can believe in himself enough to give love the chance to
     grow and flourish
Without cutting down the flowers before their first bloom.

Can such love ever last?
Is it too strong, too passionate, too perfect for this world?
Must it always be a moment in time, a mere memory?

Will there ever be another
Who loves me with such passion but no pain?
With a love as beautiful but enduring
Can it happen?

Will there ever be another who loves me like he did?

Will there ever be another?

Separation

The days since I felt your touch
Are fast disappearing into the distance.
Your voice is fading
And the contours of your face
Are becoming more blurred.

The vibrant colours
Of the pictures
Of our time together
Are becoming
Less defined.

As time moves on
And we're parted.

Yet in spite of
Or because of
The time and miles of separation
The feelings grow stronger
The bond becomes deeper
As our love fills us to overflowing.............

Our Tapestry

You pulled away destroying us
I wouldn't let you go
I clung onto the beautiful threads
Beginnings of a multicoloured tapestry – of US.

Our thoughts, feelings, secrets,
The laughter and special moments
Interwoven with sunlight, sparkling eyes, and hope for the
    future.

You walked away
And it was as if you leapt across an abyss so wide
And stood on the other side
Still silently smiling.

For weeks I balanced on the tightrope there
Step by step risking death's jaws, trying to reach you.
Carrying the precious tapestry
Oh so carefully in my hands.

One false move
And I would have fallen.
The patchwork of possibilities,
The tender connections
Of embroidered potential
Lost forever.

Sometimes you reached your hand out, helped me.
Sometimes you turned your head away
And I stood motionless
Not daring to move for fear of falling.
The darkness below loomed ever closer.

Desperately I held the tapestry up for you to see.
Hoping that
The brightness of its beauty,
The lightness of its laughter,
The excitement of its passion,
The depth of its love,
Would cause you to turn your face back to me
And then I could continue the journey.

But the last time
The back of your head was all I could see
Silhouetted against all hope
As you walked away.

My wishes laced with tears
Vanished
As the crystal cloth finally fell from my hands
Into the void below.

Without You

The pattern on the quilt cover reads passionate tender love-
    making
The last time.
I see it every day.
The light flashes on the answerphone – but it's never you.
I eagerly await the post
Drowning in disappointment.
Wine has no taste when not from your lips
My reflection so lonely in the sky-light
The bath has grown to fill the room
No one to share the moments.

CDs remain silent, photos stay hidden, places too painful to
    visit.
And in my home you pervade every space,
Every chair, every inch, I see you everywhere
I look.

Food has lost its taste
Jokes no longer funny
Even the candle flames are dim
Without you.

There's no one to share poems or brain-dump about the
    working day.

No one to cry with or laugh with or hug or cuddle or get
angry at or discuss with or ask things or tell things or eat with
or walk with or share things or read to or massage or meditate
with or kiss or make love to.

No one to lean on or look after
No one to love.

Well, there are lots of people to love
But none of them are you.
I miss you
          So very much.

We Are Both His Other Woman

I am not the other woman
She is not the wife who fails to understand him
I am not his secret mistress
She is not the most important part of his life
I am his English passion
She is his Irish public wife

I am his only soul–mate
She is his only rock
I am his dream
She is his security
I am his sexual ecstasy
She is his comfort zone
I am his spiritual partner
She is his family roots
I am his challenge
She is his safety
I am all that he ever dreamed of
She is the history he cannot leave behind
I am his greatest love and his greatest fear
She is his routine and his even keel

I am the one and only love of his life
She is his mediocre but easy life.

Untouchable Love

Untouchable love; our love
The world cannot blemish it.
Though our boat has battled through storms
And rocks have bored holes in the hull
We have not sunk.

Though angry flames have leapt around our bodies and singed
    our clothes
In moments we've healed the scars with stroking fingertips.

Though human emotions have thrown boulders between us
In seconds they've disintegrated to sand which falls from our
    entwined form as we embrace.

Untouchable love; our love
As we rise above the earthly hurts and fears and jealousies,
The mess of humanity in relationships.

Soul mates
We seek that pure simple love – agape
In our depths wanting only the best
For the other, equal to self.

Always aiming for Unconditional love
We almost reach it
After all we're still human
Not yet angels.

Special Light

I wanted to hold you
      and kiss you
      and touch you
      tonight.
It wasn't allowed.

The yearning tore at my heart
as I smiled and chatted pleasantly.
My face and head were transparent
Love and intimacy dancing in my eyes for all to see.
I daren't look into yours.

"I'm sleeping with your husband and wishing you a good
    holiday."
Lies flowing from my lips, not practised but newly formed.
What a tangled web………

You've whisked me away on a tide of attention and passion.
Your arms embrace and envelope me
As if I never need to think again.
You say I am a precious flower
And as you hold me I feel special, nurtured and safe.
Beautiful inside.

Trying to foresee the future
Stomach tightens
I feel physically ill.

I can see (to quote a phrase)
It reaching its natural conclusion
And I can see
An unending future together too.

We cannot know
We must not know
This moment is the only time there is.

Growing, learning, loving
We move forward on our own unique journey.

I know our lives will touch again
As they have before

And there'll always be a
Special light between us.

So Much More Time

Don't say it has to end yet.
So many things to tell you and show you
So much of life to share with you
So many places to go
So many questions to ask.
I want so much more time.

The clock always ticking
Time's winged chariot

I dream of days and nights together
When the minutes don't matter
And we float on a tide of love and laughter.
Ebbing and flowing from playfulness to passion, romance to
    reason
Love to logic, bedroom to beach.

I want so much more time
Don't say it has to end yet.
So much more time.

Chapter Three – Haikus

Haiku originates from the Japanese short poem of three lines; five syllables, seven syllables, five syllables. It can be poignant to create a whole image or feeling with very few words.

Haikus from Abroad

Hospital Haikus

Enlightenment

Norfolk Haikus

Haikus about Love

Sudoku Haikus

Ten Minutes on the Drive

Cancer Haiku

Haikus From Abroad

In a Foreign Place
Amidst the concrete
A tree stands with oranges
Does it belong here?

Glasses of cool wine
Filled our veins with confidence
Later we asked why.

Days of endless sun
We kissed and danced and laughed long
Must it ever end?

We opened our hearts
And poured out our souls' longing
Kindred spirits found.

The flame of passion
Burned brightly between our legs.
A harsh drug to us.

Hospital Haikus

In Hospital
Lights bleepers loud noise
Curtains commodes – a false world
When will I get out?

Your Visit
The touch of your hand
Soothes the pain and fear away
Reminds me of life.

At My Bedside
As you stroke my leg
You're speaking of Tuscany
Transported we fly.

Bucklesham Room 9
The room is quieter
Yet I'm still in so much pain
When will it all end?

5 a.m.
Panic and shaking
Mind and body in turmoil
Where is the meaning?

Hospital Life
The endless waiting
No control over my life
Reality gone.

No Shower
All choices seem gone
Everything takes forever
I want my life back.

Enlightenment

The crash of the waves
Sun glistening with whiter foam
My soul has come home.

The crash of the waves
I breathe in the tide of life
I am all that is.

The crash of the waves
To keep this song in my heart
I'll always fly high!

Norfolk Haikus

Walking on the beach
At Brancaster in winter
Arm in loving arm

Cuddling here with you
Warm snuggling under white sheets
Away from the world.

I like to snuggle
I like to cuddle with you
Send the world away

Sticky marmalade
Cake beside a roaring fire
Poetry with tea.

Haikus about love

Here in My Life

Laying down to rest
Missing you floods my being
Why are we apart?

In the Golden Sunshine

Sparkling sea ripples.
Sitting, a space at my side.
I'm missing you so.

Our Special Place

Sea sounds sights and sun
Soak like salt through our senses
As soul-mates we're home.

The Bedroom

I look around me
There's no trace of you left here
But in my heart you shine.

Love Living – Living Love

As the years roll by
Let's celebrate each moment
And love living now.

As the years roll by
Let's celebrate each moment
Live a life of love!

Sudoku Haikus

Don't interrupt me
Frustrated concentration
Where will the three go?

He can't speak to me
Addicted to the puzzle
Sudoku widow.

Ten Minutes on the Drive
Always sitting now
Blankets cold wind and hot tea
More freedom outside.

Cancer Haiku

Great news, scan all clear!
This gift of life is for you.
Now what will you do?

Chapter Four – The Challenges of the Soul

The gift of life brings many challenges; illness, pain, anger, frustration. It is all part of being human.

Living with M.E.

My Anger

Trapped by M.E.

Oh Let Me Be Me!

Angel on Earth

The Lie

God Nervous God Breakdown God

The Alfred Corry

I'm Ok

Thank You and I Hurt

How to Accept

Living With M.E.

The struggle
Wading through treacle
Vainly seeking normality
A circus of symptoms
As they each take their turn
But never leave the ring
Unending spiralling.

Slow life at stand – still
Observe each bud appear and open
On the tree each branch is known intimately
So familiar.

No far off exciting adventures
Plane rides or hot sun
No clear warm waters
Exotic food and fish
Foreign tongue.

My world has shrunk
One town
One house
One room
One bed

Yet time to sit and stare
I see the whole world
In a single daffodil.

My Anger

My anger is a raging torrent
Battering boats into pieces against sharp rocks.
A storm lashing rain into faces
Whipping bare skin until it bleeds.
Biting cold howling wind
Snow blizzards and tornadoes
Destroying lives in its daily toil.

My anger is a volcano
Erupting with burning hot red racing lava
Devouring whole cities in its wake.

The piercing sun
Perishing and withering all life.
A wolf's sharp fangs dripping blood after the kill
A tiger's roar chasing its prey
The Devil's eyes filled with hate.

My anger is more fierce than the strongest predator killer
More powerful than a tsunami
More deadly than fatal poison
As vast
As the darkest deepest most infinite void.

Trapped by M.E.

Trapped in this body
I want to walk, to step out boldly, to march, to skip, to dance,
    to run, to jump, to hop, to swim.
I want to fly!

Trapped in this body
Trying to calm the storm inside me
My heart races like battering rain
Stomach churns like waves
Crashing violently onto the rocks.

Trapped in this body
That won't work as it should.

Tight pain in my chest, no breath
Burning , no strength
Spinning head, shaking – panic
Thoughts that refuse to find their vocal words
I become unintelligible.
Internal thermometer broken down.

Yet the picture outside is calm – no violent waves there
Watery winter sun
The sea stretches to the horizon like a flat prairie plain
Small sparkling ripples punctuate the ocean.

Like moments of calm
                clarity
                animation
                strength
Then disappear in a blink.

The sun streams diagonal lines from cloudland to sea-scape.
Free falling…………..
Oh let me escape
from this body
and feel peace like that again.

Oh Let Me Be Me!

Oh let me be me!
Let me find out through this multi-coloured tunnel of time
What that means.
Let me feel it and know it
So that this long journey of pain and confusion
Can end
And the real journey begin.

Let those flashes, those twinklings, those sparks, which have
    sometimes forced their way out
Now come bursting forth
In a great bright blazing torrent.
A flood of passionate me!

And let this me
Continue to grow
Becoming myself as I travel through life
Finding my own true expression in this world.

Able to give more, accept more, feel more, be more, love more
Because the whole of me is free.
No part suppressing another
No inner conflict and confusion.

Let me love and accept myself totally as I am.
Then
At last I can be me!

Angel On Earth

Her eyes smile with sparkle
And she breathes through the pain,
As they tell her the news
That she won't walk again.

She'll never throw a ball or lift a drink
To her lips,
She'll never wash her own face at the sink
Or put her hands on her hips.

Her toes will never feel
The cool ripple of the sea,
Her hands won't hold again
Her own front door key.

Yet she smiles for her children,
Listens to friends when they phone,
She praises their achievements,
And listens to them moan.

Not an ounce of resentment,
Not a trace of envy
Flickers across her face,
No sign of jealousy.

If it were me I'd scream and shout
"What the hell is MY life about?
You carry on as normal, complaining though you're free
And no-one understands what it's really like for me!"

But with the grace of an angel,
She listens like a saint
To the stories of their lives,
The pictures that they paint.

A soldier, a fireman, a lion,
Are not as brave as she,
Heaven sent from a higher realm,
Teaching us humility.

Giving love eternally,
We glimpse immortality.

The Lie

It was so small and insignificant
A white lie, don't they say?
It slipped easily into the conversation almost unnoticed
Like the family pet entering the room to settle by the fire.

With a start!
I saw through its disguise
And felt it pierce at the very core of my knowledge of you.
A sharp wound
A ridge between us.

Shocked and shaken, my certainty reeled
A jumble of facets jostling for their true place
An order I thought I'd known.
So many parts of you, your life, where I'm less than a novice
Can't even be a spectator
But our togetherness is the one certain strong stability.
Our honesty, our empathy, our deep knowing of each other
Our truth
Bare naked truth
The foundation of our intimacy.

Soulmates Don't Lie

Is this the tiny drop of venom
That poisons our innocence?
Are we to watch the badness
Seep into the veins of our togetherness?
Until love becomes encrusted with bitterness and distrust?
And beauty disintegrates
Into sharp pieces of broken glass?

God Nervous God Breakdown God

Tangles of confusion
Whirlpools of which way to go
But no way seems open
Only down and down.
Despair and desperately crying
"My God, my God, why hast thou forsaken me?"
Piercing nails through my mind
Wishing for the sweet release of tears.
"I thirst"–
But the water has long since dried.

No rest, no comfort, no emotion
Body shakes yet devoid of all energy
Feverish, the tension builds, hot, cold, pounding heart, I must
    be going to die.
But no, the gates open
As I cry and cry and cry.

No reason
Yet the tortures of my soul will not cease.
So many comforting souls.
Why can't they love it away?

Many times I've seen the light
The sun has streamed through the mountain tops–
Certain I've made it.
And then the ground has been moved
From beneath my feet again
And I fall deeper and deeper into murky waters.
When will the hurt be over?
When will I find out why?
Suddenly, with the peaks on the graph of my existence

I understand the words of a song;
"Today we'll see the butterflies
We'll smell the grass
And we'll feel the skies.
What a day – let no-one take this away."
Whatever pain, suffering, despair
Tomorrow or yesterday may hold
This beautiful poignant moment
That has been given to me
Is mine to share and give thanks for
Is mine for eternity.

Knowing it's all for a reason.
Gradually as the mist rolls away
A new picture emerges before my eyes.
Clearer, brighter and more beautiful
Than the old one which was there before.
The water is still.
Not through indifferent passivity
But deep inner calm.

As I pass through the days
And the pain gradually fades away
I know that when I hit the depths
I was carried all the way.

Now walking alone through deserted streets
Walking tall, the spirit in me.
Every shadow now has a brightness
Every scowl becomes a smile.
Thank you God for showing me
That although we can cling to our loved ones
In the end we must rest ourselves
Entirely on Thee.

The Alfred Corry

Four years later,
We return to that shed
Where, standing beside her,
We had heard tales
Of bravery, storms and lives saved.

She was neglected and rotting
Barely saved from ruin.
Now she has been restored;
Smooth wood, lovingly crafted,
To rebuild her strength and lines.

I have had my own shipwreck,
Body collapsed, timbers rotting,
Rescued, like her, from stormy waters.
Now I must sit to hear.
But looking up at her
Becoming her former self,
She is an inspiration to my own restoration.

The *Alfred Corry* was a sailing lifeboat built in 1893. She served at Southwold in Suffolk for 25 years and saved many lives. In 1919 she became a yacht and had 14 different owners. Now she is back home, only 300 yards from where she was first launched. She is being returned to her original form, and is housed in a restored lifeboat shed dating from 1922.

I'm Ok

Whilst others ooze excitement, ecstasy.
They're in love!
They've won the lottery!
I remain calm, level-headed.
My trip around the world?
"It was ok", I say.

They rave about their holiday.
New job, new car, new baby.
Adrenaline pumping through their veins.
My new house?
"It's quite nice," I say.

Promotion leaves me cold.
Parties I'd rather miss.
Meals are for eating not enthusing.
Fireworks still exist without **MY** ooing and ahhing.

They've cheated death, conquered cancer, found Jesus!
"I'm happy for you, really I am."
But after the earthquake,
All I can say,
Is "I'm ok……..thank-you."

Some say I'm boring, unfeeling or a fool.
Maybe I'm missing out?
But when they're at the bottom in despair,
I'm in the mediocre mundane middle,
Still sitting there.
I'm safe.
I'm ok.

Thank You and I Hurt

Thank you for daffodils, blazing, waving in the breeze
My eyes see them but my heart stays closed

Thank you for my garden
My body shakes

Thank you for my partner, family, friends, my cat
My legs are so weak

Thank you for my house and living by the sea
My heart feels heavy

Thank you for birdsong, flowers, trees, the air we breathe
Tortured by symptoms my life feels futile

Thank you for music and kisses and playing with children
Panic overwhelms me

Thank you for this amazing world
Let me feel part of it again.

Thank you for my life
Can this time of pain pass quickly?

So I can be me
And love life again.

How to Accept?

How to accept?
When it feels like torture.
The ceaseless shaking, quaking
Five a.m waking
Adrenaline pumping
Fight or flight so strong
But where is the tiger?
But where is the lion?

It's only a physical sensation
And it will pass
Face, accept, float, let time go by.
When panic goes
Fatigue so strong.
I become a prisoner in my house.
Impossible choice
Paralysed by fatigue or tortured by panic.

Accept the physical
Accept the spiritual
If it's happening, it has to be perfect
In the grand plan.

How to trust in the process?
Such a big shift needed.
How to love what is?
Loving even this?

Only with acceptance
Can there be transformation.
Trusting and staying positive
Letting go of yearning

Shifting from all I believed I wanted.
Peace of mind and gratitiude.

And the prize – so great!
The joy of living
Connection to spirit
When we love what is.

So, this is the Honours paper
A PhD in trust
In loving what is.

Seems impossible
But it's the only way.
No choice but this.
No giving up
Keep asking for help
Keep moving towards
Acceptance.

Step by step
Bit by bit
A minute here
A moment there.
Through immobility
Through pain
I've done it before
I can do it!

Chapter Five – The Joy of the Soul

Connecting to the deep centre of love within our soul brings peace. It is Agape, not Ego love. More constant and unconditional than a human physical love.

The Promised Land

Come
Step onto the shore
Take my hand
Leave the storm clouds behind
Join me in the Promised Land.

Let us dance amongst the daffodils
Let us run hand in hand through poppy-laden meadows
Let us roll in the sweet smelling grass
And lie on our backs soaking up the sun as we look out into
    the blue yonder.
Forever summertime
In our land of love.

We'll swim with the fish and fly with the birds
We'll play with the butterflies
And laugh until our bellies ache
We'll count the stars
And sing until our hearts reach Heaven.

Come
Step onto the shore
Take my hand
I can't dive into the stormy sea to reach you
I live here
In the Promised Land.

There's A Deep Peace

There's a deep peace
Waiting inside us
There's a deep peace
Waiting for you.

Pull back the curtains of catastrophic thinking
Strip away self-doubt
Let go of conflict, fear, and hurt
Release anger
Move beyond physical pain.

There's a deep peace
Waiting to be revealed
A moment of knowing
A moment that can last forever
When we see with eyes anew from on high.

Transcendental Experience

Part One

Suddenly
My love for you reached a new level
Found a new understanding
Encompassed a new depth.
I didn't have to try.
It just was.
The ego moved away and revealed the soul.
What bliss!
The ego with its hanging on, its jealousy, its possessiveness, its
    wanting everything its way, its trying to mould the object of
    its love into what it needs for itself.
What bliss to be rid of it for a while!

My love for you became one with the Universe
And I was overwhelmed with such compassion and empathy
    for your ego state of pain
And gradually that feeling dissolved into................
Soul love
Unconditional
Agape
I saw the sheer beauty of your soul shining brightly beneath
    the pain and confusion.
I saw your real self in all its glory revealed to me – perfect.

Tears sprang to my eyes.
Not tears of pain
But tears of beauty, truth and pure love.
As I felt as never before.
Words cannot come near to express the feeling.

I loved you so much that I didn't need to keep you, have you,
    change you.
I really could let you go.
At that moment I wanted you to be happy more than I wanted
    you for myself.
I could allow you to be you.
I stood back in wonder at the process.

Part Two

The love for you
The Soul love
Connected me to timeless ecstacy.
Sparked off an experience
Beyond all words, all thoughts, all feelings.
I was filled with golden light
So full of love that I merged with the whole world.
I became the trees, the sky, the cars, the shops, the people.
I wanted to hug every person I saw…………
I was an angel sprouting wings
I could fly.
The world was more real
The colours more vivid
And yet none of it mattered
I was The One.

A Moment Of Truth

The warmth of your embrace
The closeness of your breathing
Arms around encompassing our hearts
As their beat becomes a unison.

Breathing in and out in harmony
We are as embryos in the womb
We are as newborn beings in the world
At the very core of life itself
So simple
         We belong.

I AM

I am the bubbling laughter of existence
I am giggling creation
I am all that is, was, and ever will be
I am everyone and everything
I am the wind, the sea, the air, all creatures, all beings
I am a shining star
I am the Universe.

I am a spark of light, of love
I join with all of space and grow in vastness and beauty
I AM the whole of creation
I AM the Universe
I AM Source
I AM the Infinite.
Not a part of it, but the whole of it
I give birth to all life
All life comes through me
Is from me
Is a part of me
All life IS me
I am all of life.

I have no personality
Because I am ALL personalities.
All ideas, beliefs, desires, fall away
Because
I am already All that there is.
I am every idea, every belief
I am everything.
There is nothing left which is not me.

How can I desire to have anyone?
I already AM everyone.
How can I desire to bring forth life?
I have already created everyone and everything.
How can I desire anything?
I already AM everything.
I AM GOD.
Not only a spark of the Infinite
But the whole of God.
Pure Love, Grace, gentleness in expression
Lightness and bubbling laughter
Being the Infinite is fun!

It's all one great Loving joke.
The joke is believing WE are important personalities
That our little fears, needs and desires are real.

God is laughing
In the kindest way.
I am bubbling over with laughter and tears.
It's big, and it's all fun and light and easy
One great big Loving pure giggle.
Like a child building a model, creating a playworld
In which to experience Outrageous Joy!

My true self is the Vast Loving Infinite
And the Infinite finds it all fun!

A Miracle

Greys turn to full technicolour
Every person is glowing with love
The sun shines through the pouring rain.

I am part of the whole
Dancing through life
Suddenly it's all so easy
No trying anymore.

Present in the moment
Seconds flow into minutes into hours into days
Each morning I awake with the excitement of life
No ordinary moments.

The open tulip, the cat's antics, a solitary singing black bird,
A spider spinning its web, the friendly stranger.
But also zen in the washing up, beauty in the storm cloud,
Fun in the traffic jam,
The gift of learning
In the pain of illness.

The joy of living

       When I finally learn

              To love what is.

Take Your Chance

Take your chance for happiness and love
Gather it up in your arms like mountains of daffodils
And run with it
Run like the wind
Through fields of golden corn
Over carpets of lilac heather
Across vast sandy beaches
Past green trees of dappled sunlight
Keep on running
And hold on to your treasure.

Don't drop it through fear
Or let it go through lack of courage
Or lose it through indecision
Or watch it disappear as you focus on your insecurities.

Instead, follow the path where your heart leads
Have faith
Leave your fears behind like a trail of black smoke
Move forward to manifest your own happiness
Take a chance
Be brave and strong
You'll never pass the same path again
You may regret
If you pass it by
You'll never know
If it could have been
Your heaven on earth.

Pebble

Precious Pebble, my furry friend
So blessed to have you for so long
Fun, joy, companionship, comfort, love
Sent to help my healing
You opened my heart to more love.

Stability during the years of many men
At my side during the long days of bed rest
On my lap as I progressed to drive around the garden
Always here
Always with me.

Your rough tongue on my finger, licking crème fraiche
Silky soft warm comfort of your fur
Healing vibration of your gentle purr
Sense of calm as I stroke you
Carefree chasing the laser light in circles
Sunbathing with me
Bridge, play readers, piano lessons
You joined in them all
You must be Grade 5 piano by now!

The 'Good Morning' meows as I opened my bedroom door
The 'welcome' meows as I returned home
The 'hurry up and get into evening position' meows as I
    worked on the computer
The 'give me some crème fraiche' meows as I ate my fruit.

The house is so quiet and empty now
There's a big space where you were
I expect to see you as I come in the back door

I think I hear you as I open a tin of tuna
My lap is so empty in the evening
But I feel your love in my heart.

Such a great love, so unconditional
Such a wise soul, loved by so many
Reminding me to savour each moment, love what is, life is a
    gift
Connect to spirit, love myself
We are all love.

Run free dear Pebble, released from your aching body
Returned to spirit from whence you came
The love we shared will never end.